THE FACTS ON THE KING JAMES ONLY DEBATE

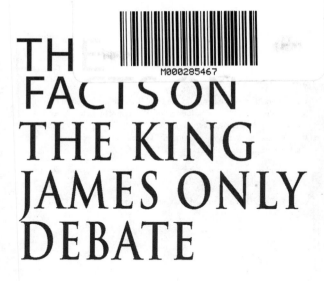

JOHN ANKERBERG
& JOHN WELDON

HARVEST HOUSE™ PUBLISHERS

EUGENE, OREGON

Cover by Terry Dugan Design, Minneapolis, Minnesota

THE FACTS ON THE KING JAMES ONLY DEBATE

Copyright © 1996 by the Ankerberg Theological Research Institute
Published by Harvest House Publishers
Eugene, Oregon 97402

Library of Congress Cataloging-in-Publication Data

Ankerberg, John, 1945-
  The facts on the King James only debate / John Ankerberg and John Weldon.
    p. cm. — (Facts on series)
Originally published: Eugene, Or. : Harvest House, ©1996.
Includes bibliographical references.
  ISBN 0-7369-1111-1 (pbk.)
  1. Bible. English—Versions—Authorized. I. Weldon, John. II. Title.
BS186 .A54 2003
220.5'2038—dc21   2002010768

Printed in the United States of America

03 04 05 06 07 08 09 / VP-KB / 10 9 8 7 6 5 4 3 2 1

CONTENTS

Directory of Bible Versions Cited

ASV: American Standard Version
Goodspeed
JB: Jerusalem Bible
KJV: King James Version
MLB: Modern Language Bible (Berkeley)
Moffatt
NAB: New American Bible
NASB: New American Standard Bible
NEB: New English Bible
NIV: New International Version
NKJV: New King James Version
RV: Revised Version
RSV: Revised Standard Version
TEV: Today's English Version
TLB: The Living Bible

THE MOST IMPORTANT
BOOK OF HISTORY

[The Bible has] played a special role in the history and culture of the modern world....The Bible brought its view of God, the universe, and mankind into all the leading Western languages and thus into the intellectual processes of Western man.... The Bible...has been the most available, familiar, and dependable source and arbiter of intellectual, moral, and spiritual ideals in the West. Millions of modern people who do not think of themselves as religious live nevertheless with basic presuppositions that underlie the biblical literature. It would be impossible to calculate the effect of such presuppositions on the changing ideas and attitudes of Western people with regard to the nature and purpose of government, social institutions, and economic theories (*Encyclopedia Britannica*).

The Bible is clearly the most important book in human history. Samuel Taylor Coleridge wrote that the best and wisest of men have born witness to its great influences in civilization, law, science, and morality and "have declared it to be beyond compare the most perfect instrument of humanity." President Ulysses S. Grant spoke of our debt to the Bible "for all the progress made in true civilization"; I. Friedlander noted its system of morality "has become the cornerstone of human civilization." Abraham Lincoln called it "the best gift God has given to man," while Patrick Henry said "it is worth all other books which were ever printed." William Gladstone noted that "an immeasurable distance separates it from all competitors," and Rousseau commented, "The majesty of the Scriptures astonishes me." Kant declared, "The Bible is the greatest benefit which the human race has ever experienced" and "a single line in the Bible has consoled me more than all the books I ever read besides." Isaac Newton regarded "the Scriptures of God the most sublime philosophy," and Henri De Lubac wrote,

"The Bible makes an extraordinary impression on the historian.…No where else can be found anything in the least like it." Perhaps such accolades underscore why A.M. Sullivan observed, "The cynic who ignores, ridicules or denies the Bible, spurning its spiritual rewards and aesthetic excitement, contributes to his own moral anemia."[1]

The Christian church does indeed possess a marvelous treasure; honoring it before the world is a privilege. Not surprisingly, no subject is more important for the Christian than the Bible. Every Christian who reads it knows that the Scripture claims to be the divinely inspired and inerrant Word of God. This means that the inspired Scriptures comprise God's very own words to us and that they do not contain even a single error. The Lord Jesus Christ told us this when He stated, "Thy word is truth" (John 17:17, KJV). The Scripture itself declares it is "perfect," "very pure," and "sacred" (see Psalm 19:7; 119:140; 2 Timothy 3:15, NASB). We are told by God Himself that the Scriptures can never be destroyed; they are irrevocable. Jesus said, "The scripture cannot be broken" (John 10:35). He also said, "heaven and earth shall pass away, but my words shall not pass away" (Matthew 24:35, KJV), for "it is easier for heaven and earth to pass away than for one stroke of a letter of the Law to fail" (Luke 16:17, NASB). The apostle Peter emphasized that the living and abiding word of God is imperishable (see 1 Peter 1:23, NASB). The prophet Isaiah cried out, "The grass withereth, the flower fadeth: but the word of our God shall stand for ever" (Isaiah 40:8, KJV).

So how did we get our Bible, this most influential book in human history? God directly inspired those who wrote it. The apostle Paul emphasized, "All scripture is given by inspiration of God" (2 Timothy 3:16, KJV). The apostle Peter told us the process by which such divine inspiration occurred. Those specific individuals who actually wrote "the very words [logia] of God" (Romans 3:2, NIV) were "holy men of God [who] spake as they were moved by the Holy Ghost" (2 Peter 1:21, KJV). As the NIV puts it, "prophecy never had its origin in the will of man, but men spoke from God as they were carried along by the Holy Spirit" (2 Peter 1:21). Here, Peter employs a highly instructive word, *pheromene*, which was used of a ship carried along by the wind. As Edwin A. Blum points out, this Scripture "remarkably clarifies the cooperation of the dual authors of Scripture."[2] The Holy Spirit filled the original writers of Scripture and "carried them along" in the direction He wished so that even though men actually wrote the words of Scripture, they were the very words that God Himself inspired and wanted to be written down for posterity.

This explains the position of the Christian church for 20 centuries: Only the *original* writings by the inspired authors, those who first penned the 66 books of the canon of the Bible, are the actual, inerrant Word of God. In other words, collectively, as soon as these individuals stopped writing, the canon of the Bible was complete and divine revelation ended. From that point on, in order to have God's Word, Christians had to make *copies* of the original, divinely inspired manuscripts.

Today, even though we do not possess the original autographs (the actual parchments or papyri that Scripture was first written on), and even though meaningful variant readings (copyists differences) exist for about one or two percent of the Bible, we can still know that the copies—collectively taken— give us 100 percent of the original manuscripts. This means nothing has been lost of God's original inspiration and that we retain 100 percent of the inerrant Word of God.

Even the degree of variation between the two manuscripts that differ the most of the 5300 we possess "would not fundamentally alter the message of the Scriptures."[3] In the small area where word differences among copyists do exist, textual critics of the Bible attempt to determine the most probable original reading.

This means that Christians can fully trust their Bibles. If 1) the extant copies of manuscripts can be shown to be 99 percent original, and 2) the remaining inconsequential one percent still contains the original among the variants, then there is no reason to doubt we have the inerrant Word of God as the prophets and apostles delivered it to us. (This kind of research and degree of manuscript authenticity occurs only in Judaism and Christianity. No other major religion in the world can logically establish the authenticity of their scriptures in terms of both divine inspiration and manuscript preservation.[4])

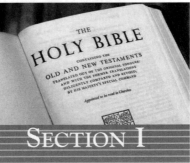

SECTION I

The King James Bible

1

What are the basic issues involved in the King James Only (KJO) debate?

Some Christians today believe that the King James Version (KJV) of the Bible is the only legitimate Bible. Furthermore, like the original writings or "autographs" of Scripture, they believe that only the KJV is inspired and inerrant (without error).

There are several distinct KJV groups which include: 1) people who prefer the KJV above all other Bibles but could not be classified as KJV only; 2) people who argue that the underlying Hebrew and Greek texts used by the KJV translators are superior to all other texts. This group would not necessarily argue that such texts are inspired but that they more accurately reflect the original writings; 3) those who argue that only the Textus Receptus (TR) has been supernaturally preserved and inspired and is therefore inerrant. (The TR is the text on which the KJV was based; there are over 30 editions, none 100 percent identical.) For those who hold this view, the KJV translation itself would not necessarily be inspired; 4) the most dominant group are those who argue that the KJV translation itself constitutes an inspired and inerrant text. Categories 3 and 4 comprise the core of the controversy and are our principal concern.

Sadly however, the KJO controversy is a pseudo-issue largely based on false arguments. Therefore it is not an issue the church should have to deal with. But it is one the church has been forced to address; indeed, church splits have happened as a direct consequence of KJO writings: "Responsibility must be laid at the door of the KJV Only camp for the destruction of many a good Christian Church in America and abroad."[5]

The majority of perceived problems raised by new translations arise from two sources: 1) from misconceptions about the KJV, and 2) lack of understanding regarding the origin and transmission of the Bible (including the nature of translation work and the textual data we possess).

Indeed, D.A. Carson (Ph.D., Cambridge University) points out that the degree of uncertainty raised by textual questions (what is actually in the manuscripts) is a great deal less than the degree of uncertainty raised by how one interprets what the manuscripts say:

> In other words, even when the text is certain, there is often an honest difference of opinion among interpreters as to the precise meaning of the passage. Few Evangelicals, I would like to think, will claim infallibility for their interpretations of the Scriptures; they are prepared to live with the (relatively) small degree of uncertainty raised by such limitations. The doubt raised by textual uncertainties, I submit, is far, far smaller.[6]

Expressing the kind of concern that the KJO people do over one percent of the text, when this one percent does not deal in important matters, is like risking your life to save $100 million already safely in the bank. Further, the relevance of the one to two percent can't compare with the unfortunate divisiveness caused by this debate.

In essence, the KJO debate concerns three basic issues: 1) evaluating the "families" of manuscripts (deciding whether it is the minority of earliest manuscripts or the majority of late manuscripts that are closer to the originals); 2) determining the best text, i.e., how we ascertain the original words among all the manuscripts we possess (this concerns the one to two percent relevant variant readings); and 3) producing a good translation—accurately translating the Greek and Hebrew words that are established and the methods brought to the translating process (whether the members of the translation committees translated properly and the degree to which one sacrifices a strict literal translation in order to translate the meaning more accurately and, hence, enhance the understanding of Scripture).

Points one and two involve textual variants. An example of a textual variant can be found in John 6:47 where the KJV reads, "He that believeth *on me* hath everlasting life" (italics added). Modern translations read, "He who believes has eternal life," the words "on me" not being present. The reason they are not present is because they are not found in the earliest manuscripts. But contextually, the meaning is exactly the same even if the words "on me" are not in the verse. In the immediate and larger contexts, it is clear that the term "on me" is implied. So this kind of textual variant does not change the meaning.

An example of a translational difference can be found in John 3:36 where the KJV reads, "He that *believeth not* the Son shall not see life," whereas the NASB reads, "He who *does not obey* the Son shall not see life" (italics added). Are we dealing with unbelief or disobedience? Are there any implications for the doctrine of salvation by grace through faith alone? At issue is how to properly translate the single Greek word *apeitheo* that is found in John 3:36. This term can be translated as either unbelief or disobedience. To illustrate, the KJV translates the same word, *apeitheo*, as disobedience in other places such as 1 Peter 3:1 (obey not); 4:17 (obey not); and Romans 2:8 (do not obey).

The main reason modern translations translate the term as "disobey" is because this is the primary meaning of the term. Most words have multiple meanings but usually one is primary or the most common meaning. The KJV translation of "disbelief" is a secondary translation by extension—not the direct, primary translation. The KJV is not mistranslating the term because it is a possible translation. But it is not giving the most literal usage.[7] Regardless, this is not a major issue concerning the nature of salvation as KJO proponents argue since "there is no conflict between obedience to Christ and belief in Christ. True faith is obedience to Christ" because a "disobedient faith" is a nonentity. "Just because there are those who might misuse the term 'obey' so as to promote a works-salvation viewpoint does not in any way change the meaning of the term itself."[8]

2

Is the KJO position established by the history of the KJV?

Many KJO writers argue God had the KJV written so that, through the translators, He could produce an inerrant English Bible. In fact, it was written for a far more mundane reason: to produce a good standard translation that would be most acceptable to all concerned. Understanding the background of the KJV will help us comprehend the issues involved.

How did we get the KJV? The KJV Bible was first published in 1611, and subsequent printings or editions corrected a number of translation errors (this occurred in 1612, 1613, 1616, 1629, 1638, 1660, 1683, 1727, 1762, 1769, and 1873). What this means is that each one of these versions differed in certain places from the previous edition. (In fact, there were two slightly different 1611 editions and six slightly different editions in the 1650s.[9])

There are even a few significant differences between the 1611 edition and our modern version. In 1611, the KJV had "Then cometh Judas" in Matthew 26:36. Today it is rendered in the KJV as, "Then cometh Jesus." Wouldn't everyone agree this is a rather significant difference? There were also a few embarrassing printing errors. The 1613 printing omitted the word "not" from the seventh commandment, inadvertently "encouraging" people to commit adultery. This King James edition became known as the "Wicked Bible." Another printing of the KJV became known as the "Unrighteous Bible" because it stated that the *unrighteous* will inherit the kingdom of heaven. And a few printing errors continue to occur in the KJV and other versions today.[10]

The KJV Bible we use today is actually based primarily on a major revision completed in 1769. This was 158 years after the first edition.[11] (If the *1611 edition* is the true Word of God, it is no longer in circulation. If not, which KJV edition do KJO writers wish to defend

14

as the inerrant Word of God? The editions of 1611, 1769, and the TR itself have all been advocated.)

In making the New Testament (NT) translation, the translators used the 1516 Greek text of the Catholic scholar Desiderius Erasmus. Erasmus took less than a year to produce his text, which was based on portions of only five or six late manuscripts (12–14 century). In addition, his work was produced in haste in order to be the first to actually publish a Greek NT. Not surprisingly, given the conditions under which he worked, the various editions of his text are, collectively, filled with a significant number of corrections. Both Stephanus and Beza revised his text. It is this Greek text, along with Erasmus' *Complutensian Polyglot* that was used by the translators to produce the first edition of the King James Bible (1611).

Some of the problems which Erasmus bypassed in his hasty work have been summarized by noted Princeton scholar Bruce M. Metzger:

> For most of the text he relied on two rather inferior manuscripts in the university library at Basle, one of the Gospels and one of the Acts and Epistles, both dating from about the twelfth century....[Because of back translation from Latin into Greek in a manuscript of Revelation] here and there... are readings which have never been found in any known Greek manuscript but which are still perpetuated today in printings of the so-called Textus Receptus of the Greek New Testament.

Evidence like this demonstrates that Erasmus' text, which evolved and became the basis for the Textus Receptus, "...was not based on early manuscripts, not reliably edited, and consequently not trustworthy."[12]

It was not until 1624 that the Elzevir brothers put out their own edition. In the second edition (1633) the preface claimed that it was the text "best received of all." This "received text," known as the "Textus Receptus" is the textual basis for the KJV NT; it differs from the Erasmus text in only a few hundred minor instances. In spite of Erasmus' use of only five or six relatively late manuscripts, the changes in all KJV editions were minor. For example, in the nineteenth century the American Bible Society examined six KJV editions then circulating. Of the 24,000 variants (the great majority in punctuation and some of the text), it noted "of the great number, there is not one which mars the integrity of the text or affects any doctrine or precept of the Bible."[13] This is because the King James translators had used the same basic principles employed by modern translators, and their skill and scholarship gave us what became the standard English Bible for 400 years.

3

What did the King James translators declare about their translation?

KJO proponents allege that the 1611 edition of the King James Bible is the most accurate because it is divinely inspired and therefore inerrant. Some have even argued it should be used to correct the Greek and Hebrew manuscripts we now possess.

Actually, if we examine what the KJV translators stated about their translation, the proof rests entirely *against* the KJO camp. The translators made no claims for divine inspiration; indeed, they frankly conceded theirs was *not* a perfect translation. For KJO advocates to argue otherwise is indefensible. Let's see what the KJV translators did say.*

The translators begin their preface to the reader by noting their expectation that their translation will come under unfair criticism and attack. This is something every new translation has faced historically, and modern translations, obviously, are no exception. Thus, the translators regretfully state that their attempt to provide a new and accurate translation of the Scriptures into the common English tongue will be "welcomed with suspicion instead of love, and with

---

*The following quotations are taken from "The Translators to the Reader," *The Holy Bible—1611 edition, King James Version: A Word-for-Word reprint of the First Edition of the Authorized Version* (Nashville: Thomas Nelson Publishers, 1993). We have updated seventeenth-century spellings.

emulation instead of thanks: and if there be any hole left for cavil to enter…it is sure to be misconstrued, and in danger to be condemned" (p. 1). Not surprisingly, "For eighty years after its publication in 1611, the King James Version endured bitter attacks. It was denounced as theologically unsound and ecclesiastically biased, as truckling to the king and unduly deferring to his belief in witchcraft, as untrue to the Hebrew text and relying too much on the Septuagint."[14]

But just as the editors and translators of the modern translations had as their motive the desire to place the Word of God into more readable modern English, this was the desire of the KJV translators as well. They wanted Scripture to be known and understood. Remember, as the translators themselves noted, the Word of God had been hidden from the people by the policies of the Roman Catholic Church, and there was a genuine need for a new translation in the common language. On one hand, the translators said, "we shall be traduced by Popish persons at home or abroad, who therefore will malign us, because we are poor instruments to make God's holy Truth to be yet more and more known unto the people, whom they desire still to keep in ignorance and darkness" (p. ii). On the other hand, they said, "happy is the man that delighteth in the Scripture and thrice happy that meditate in it day and night. But how shall man meditate in that which they cannot understand? How shall they understand that which is kept close [veiled] in an unknown tongue?…[Contemporary] Translation it is that opens the window, to let in the light….indeed, without translation into the vulgar [common] tongue, the unlearned are but like children at Jacob's well (which was deep) without a bucket or something to draw with…" (pp. 3,4).

So it seems the KJV translators themselves could hardly object to modern translations if both had the same purpose in mind. Recognizing they were among a long line of noble translators, it is unlikely they would object to future translations beyond their own. To argue that the KJV is the only acceptable translation seems to be unfounded in light of the statements of the very scholars who produced it. The translators expressed their gratitude to the many who went before them and "provided Translations into the vulgar for their Countrymen" including Syrian, Egyptian, Indian, Persian, French, Ethiopian, "and infinite other nations being barbarous people, translated it into their (mother) tongue" (p. 5). "Do we condemn the ancient [translations]? In no case:...we are so far off from condemning any of their labors that travailed before us in this kind...that we acknowledge them to have been raised up of God, for the building and furnishing of his Church.... Therefore blessed be they, and most honored be their name,...which help forward to the saving of souls" (p. 6).

In fact, the translators *encouraged* the people to use not only their own translation, but other translations as well in order to secure a fuller comprehension of the Scriptures. They declare that "a variety of translation is profitable for finding out the sense of the Scriptures" (p. 10). "Therefore let no man's eye be evil...neither let any be grieved...but let us rather bless God from the ground of our heart...to [allow] the [previous] translations of the Bible maturely considered of and examined. For by this means it comes to pass, that whatever is sound already...the same will shine as gold more brightly, being rubbed and polished; also, if anything be halting or superfluous, or not so agreeable to the original [Greek and Hebrew], the same may be corrected, and the truth set in place" (p. 7).

In other words, the translators not only wanted Scripture more widely known and understood, they also accepted earlier translations and sought to compare them along with the original Greek and Hebrew manuscripts in order to make a *better* translation: "Truly (good Christian reader) we never thought from the beginning, that we should need to make a new Translation, nor yet to make of a bad one a good one....But to make a good one better, or out of many good ones, one principal good one...that has been our endeavor" (p. 9). Again, the very same motives we find among modern godly translators.

The KJV translators also spoke to those who criticized them "for altering and amending our Translations so often" (p. 8). The translators responded by stating they could do little else, "if we will be sons of the truth"; "neither did we disdain to revise that which we had done, and to bring back to the anvil that which we had hammered" (p. 10). In other words, it is plain to see that the King James translators went through a process of changing and correcting their own translation to try to make it better. Obviously, if divine inspiration had been upon them, there would have been no need for this.

Another important point is that the KJV translators set marginal notes in their text, just as modern translations do. If KJO proponents have called the New KJV (NKJV) "diabolical" because it places all the variant readings of the Greek text in the footnotes, can they logically refrain from calling the KJV itself diabolical since its translators did the very same thing? These translators responded to their critics in a similar manner: "Some per adventure would have no variety of senses to be set in the margin, lest the authority of the Scriptures for deciding of controversies by that show of uncertainty should somewhat be shaken. But we hold their judgment not to be so sound in this point" (p. 10). Why? Because, they note, the important aspects of Scripture are unchanged; the variant readings concern only small matters. Thus,

> It has pleased God in his divine providence, here and there to scatter words and sentences of [a particular] difficulty and doubtfulness, not in doctrinal points that concern salvation…but in matters of less moment.… There be many words in the scriptures, which be never found there but once…so that we cannot be helped by conference of places. Again, there be many rare names of certain birds, beasts and precious stones, etc. concerning which the Hebrews themselves are so divided among themselves for judgment.…Now in such a case, does not a margin do well to admonish the Reader to seek further, and not to conclude or dogmatize upon this or that peremptorily?…[T]o determine of such things as

> the Spirit of God has left…questionable, can be no less than presumption.
>
> Therefore, as St. Augustine said, that variety of Translations is profitable for the finding out of the sense of the Scriptures: so diversity of signification and sense in the margin, where the text is not so clear, must need do good, yea, is necessary, as we are persuaded (p. 10).

Following this tradition in the NKJV, "…the textual notes are specially helpful, indicating not only where the wording differs from that of the generally accepted critical text but also where it differs from the majority text. These notes make no value judgments but enable the reader to see at a glance what the textual situation is and to assess it in the light of the context."[15]

4

Is the KJV a perfect or divinely inspired translation?

As noted, most KJO proponents claim that the KJV is perfect and without error. Dr. Samuel C. Gipp says of the 1611 KJV, "I believe the *King James Bible* is perfect" and Peter Ruckman even thinks "[so-called] mistakes in the A.V. 1611 are advanced revelation!"[16] Most KJO adherents also believe the KJV is divinely inspired. The difficulty is that the KJV has demonstrable errors. This leaves only two options: Either the KJO position is wrong or God has inspired errors.

KJO advocates usually claim that anyone who criticizes the KJV is "against God and His Word." But we have noted that even the KJV translators criticized their own translation by their subsequent corrections. In other words, to point out errors in the KJV should not be considered an attack on the Word of God but a correction in translation. Again, the KJV translators' alternate renderings in the margins prove they did not believe their translation was inerrant.

There are not a large number of errors in the KJV but they do exist, which is not surprising for a translation made some 400 years ago. For example, in Psalm

12:7 the translation, "Thou shalt keep *them*" should be "Thou shalt keep *us*." Contextually and grammatically the pronoun should refer to people, not words. Ninety-five percent of Hebrew scholars agree the KJV has made an error here.[17] In Isaiah 4:5 "canopy" is mistranslated as "defence"; in Isaiah 5:25 "refuse" is mistranslated as "torn"; in Acts 19:2 "when" is mistranslated as "since."

James White points out a number of other translation errors in the KJV, among them Mark 6:20 ("observed" should be "kept him safe" or "protected"); Acts 5:30, "and" should be "by"; James 3:2 "we offend all" should be "in many ways"; 1 Corinthians 4:4, "For I know nothing by myself" should be "For I am conscious of nothing against myself"; Isaiah 65:11, "that troop" and "unto that number" should be the literal Hebrew "Gad" and "Mani." These are translated in modern versions as "fortune" and "destiny" since Gad and Mani were the Babylonian or Assyrian gods, the God of Fortune (Gad) and the God of Destiny (Mani); 1 Kings 10:28, "linen yarn" should be the town of Kue in Egypt; 1 Chronicles 5:26, the second use of the term "and" should be "even"; and so on.[18]

White also points out that KJV mistranslation is responsible for a number of seeming contradictions in the Bible (frequently pointed out by skeptics), which do not actually exist in the Greek text (e.g., Acts 9:7 with 22:9).[19] Further, names are also problematic in the KJV since the translators sometimes used a Greek form, a Latin form, or the Hebrew form. For example, Jesus and Joshua are both names given to the same Old Testament character (Acts 7:45; Hebrews 4:8); different spellings for the same person include Cis and Kish; Noe and Noah; Kora and Core; Hosea and Osee; Isaiah and Esay; Judas, Judah, Juda, and Jude; Zera and Zarah; etc.[20] In addition, the KJV, as the translators admitted, used a large number of ways to translate the same word. "It is universally agreed that by their variety [of translating the same word] the translators confuse the reader....[For example] *dabhar* ('a word' or 'thing') is rendered by eighty-four separate English words, *panim* ('face') by thirty-four, *sim* ('to set' or 'place') by fifty-nine...*nasah* ('to lift up') by forty-six, *abhar* ('to pass over') by forty-eight, *rabh* ('much' or 'many') by forty-four, and *tobh* ('good') by forty-one. Similar variety is seen in the New Testament, where *katargein* ('to make void') appears twenty-seven times and is rendered seventeen different ways...."[21] Other examples include the Hebrew term for "turn back" (in a single grammatical form) being rendered by 60 different words.[22] In Acts 12:4, the Hebrew word for passover is actually translated Easter even though in every other place it is translated passover by the KJV, some 28 times.[23]

There are also a number of KJV translations that are actually confusing. For example, "And Mount Sinai was altogether on a smoke" (Exodus 19:18); "Thou shalt destroy them that speak leasing" (Psalm 5:6); "The ships of Tarshish did sing of thee in thy market" (Ezekiel 27:25); and, "We do you to wit of the grace of God" (2 Corinthians 8:1).[24]

Here are some examples of other KJV errors that haven't been corrected:

> "My sore ran in the night" (Psalm 77:2) should be "my hand was stretched out"...
>
> "observed him" (Mark 6:20) should be "preserved him"...
>
> "Pineth away" (Mark 9:18) should be "becomes rigid"...
>
> "Touch me not" (John 20:17)...should be "Do not keep on holding me"...
>
> "Abstain from all appearance of evil" (1 Thessalonians 5:22) should be "every form of evil"...
>
> "For in many things we offend all" (James 3:2) should be "in many things we all offend"...[25]

Examples of how archaeological or other study has clarified the meaning of some words that were unclear in 1611 include: Pharaoh Necho went "to aid" the king of Assyria, not [be] "against" him (2 Kings 23:29). Mythical animals, such as the unicorn (Deuteronomy 33:17; Psalm 22:21; Isaiah 34:7; etc.), the satyr (Isaiah 13:21; 34:14), and the cockatrice (Isaiah 11:8; 14:29; 59:5; Jeremiah 8:17) represent translations acceptable in 1611, but today these translations have either been corrected or admitted that the exact meaning is unknown. Thus, unicorns become "wild oxen," satyrs become "wild goats," a term connected with the demonic "goat idols" in Leviticus 17:7; cockatrice becomes "snake" or "viper."[26]

None of this implies the KJV is not a good and accurate translation; it only demonstrates that the KJV translators, great scholars that they were, were still fallible men who made some errors. It proves KJO defenders who argue the KJV is inerrant are wrong.[27-29]

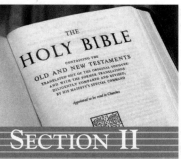

SECTION II

The KJO Position and Modern Translations

5

Do modern versions corrupt
the doctrinal purity of God's Word?

KJO proponents claim that modern versions have corrupted the doctrinal purity of God's Word and that *only* the King James Version is doctrinally sound. For example, Dr. Logsdon, David Cloud, and others assert the following: "Friends, you can say the Authorized Version (KJV) is absolutely correct. How correct? One hundred percent correct! Because biblical correctness is predicated upon doctrinal accuracy, and not one enemy of this Book of God has ever proved a wrong doctrine in the Authorized Version [AV]."[30]

Let's consider two key examples to see if a) the charge of doctrinal corruption in good modern translations is true, and b) the KJV itself is 100 percent doctrinally correct in its own translation. We will examine the key teachings of salvation by grace through faith alone and the deity of Jesus Christ.

First, proponents claim that only the KJV thoroughly defends salvation by grace through faith alone and that, in many places, the new translations actually insert salvation by good works. In chapter 15 of *New Age Bible Versions*, G.A. Riplinger claims that modern versions have conspired to dismantle salvation by faith and, instead, present a theology of works-salvation. But her arguments are false, as is easily demonstrated.[31] Riplinger claims that "verses critical to an understanding of this concept [of salvation by grace through faith] are omitted from the new version [*sic*]."[32] She proceeds to cite Romans 11:6, implying that the essential concept of salvation by grace has somehow been inaccurately portrayed in the NIV and NASB. But the NIV of Romans 11:6 reads, "And if by grace, then it is no longer by works; if it were, grace would no longer be grace." In a similar fashion, the NASB of Romans 11:6 reads, "But if it is by grace, it is no longer on the basis of works, otherwise grace is no longer grace." These verses teach salvation by grace, not by works. Nothing could be clearer. Anyone who wishes can cite dozens of verses from either the NKJV, NIV, NASB, etc., that show these Bibles clearly teach that salvation is by grace (see Ephesians 2:8,9; Galatians chapters 2–3, etc.). This suggests the alleged "conspirators" did not do a very good job.

In fact, if one uses the same logic as the KJO proponents, and cites selected passages which *seem* to teach salvation by works, one could argue that it is the *KJV itself* which distorts the doctrine of salvation. The KJV has been the favorite Bible of cults (like Mormonism) that zealously promote salvation by works. Why? Because in a number of places the KJV verses are less clear than in reliable modern versions. As White comments concerning a more general analysis, "In a majority of the passages examined...translations such as the NASB and NIV have been seen to *surpass* the KJV with reference to clarity and ease of comprehension far more often than the reverse....Most of the time a translation that differs from the KJV is just as valid and reliable as the one found in the AV itself, and at times, it is more clear and understandable."[33]

Consider another example of alleged corruption. Noting that some Catholics were involved with the Greek text of the United Bible Society (UBS), Gail Riplinger argues, "The Catholic doctrinal bend in the NIV and NASB and other new Bible [*sic*] is substantial."[34] She claims, "The Catholic teachings of salvation by works, purgatory, infant baptism...'the Virgin'...the papacy...[and] the Roman Catholic sacraments of penance, Holy Orders, and the 'Holy Eucharist'...have been sewn into the new versions...."[35] Riplinger also points out that the KJV of James 5:16 reads, "Confess your faults [*paraptoma*] one to another," and claims, "All Greek texts have the word for faults here—not sins."[36] She then points out that the new versions read, "Confess your sins" and argues or implies that the new versions not only mistranslate the word *paraptoma* but also support the Catholic sacrament of penance. But she is wrong.

First, the Greek word is correctly translated as "sins" as any Greek dictionary will prove.[37] Thus, in

Ephesians 1:7 even the KJV translates the same word (*paraptoma*) as *sins*. Second, Riplinger errs when she writes that the translation "confess your sins" supports the Catholic sacrament of penance. Christians are to confess their sins one to another. But the Catholic doctrine of penance is another teaching entirely. Penance specifically involves alleged "deadly," or mortal, sins, supposedly restores the ongoing process of justification (in a Catholic sense), and includes mandatory confession to a priest.

The truth is that not one of the Roman Catholic doctrines cited by Riplinger can be objectively and fairly shown to be taught by the NIV, NKJV, NASB, etc. Why would conservative Protestants have any desire to produce a Bible upholding unscriptural Catholic doctrines? In fact, there is little difference in word translation between official Catholic Bibles (JB/NAB, etc.) and the KJV. It is how theologians misinterpret words that cause denominational differences.

Next, KJO proponents claim that the new translations deny the biblical teaching that Jesus Christ is God. Supposedly, these new translations were written by "liberals" or "heretics" who refused to translate the truth about Christ's deity. Riplinger makes the following astounding claim, "Working 12 hours a day for nine months, comparing *every single word* in the New Testament, left me shocked and horrified at the blatant and gross omissions and perversions in new versions. I found the deity of our Lord and Savior Jesus Christ had been deleted *at every turn*."[38]

Likewise, Cecil J. Carter claims, "A characteristic of the new Bible versions is found in the way that virtually every one of them alters Scriptures which plainly teach the Deity of our Lord Jesus."[39]

Riplinger, Carter, and others claim that the NASB, NIV, NKJV, etc., are guilty of deleting the deity of Christ at many places. Riplinger refers to "over one hundred instances in which the deity of Christ is avoided."[40] In reference to Philippians 2:5-7, she claims that every new version denies the deity of Christ. She writes, "all other versions deny Christ's deity in this verse." She even says, "The NKJV, here as well as in other places, denies Christ's deity also."[41]

But, if we compare Philippians 2:6,7 in the KJV with the modern versions, we find that the deity of Christ is not denied at all; in fact, it is taught more clearly in the NIV than in the KJV. The KJV reads, "Who, being in the form of God, thought it not robbery to be equal with God." The NKJV reads the same, "Who, being in the form of God, did not consider it robbery to be equal with God." But the NIV is much clearer, "Who, *being in very nature God*, did not consider equality with God something to be grasped" (emphasis added).

Evidence of how wrong KJO promoters are can be found in Dr. D.A. Carson's book which contains a chart setting forth eight primary verses declaring that Jesus Christ is God. It examines the KJV, Revised Version, Revised Standard Version, New English Bible, Moffatt, Goodspeed, Today's English Version, NIV, Modern Language Bible, and even the Jehovah's Witnesses' *New World Translation* (NWT). Only the NWT omits all these references to Christ's deity. But even the theologically liberal translators Moffatt and Goodspeed have one and three references, respectively, ascribing deity to Christ. Significantly, the KJV is only a little better, translating *only four of the eight* verses as references to Jesus' deity. But the NIV has the highest number by far: *seven of eight references* clearly teach Christ's deity.[42]

In James R. White's fine book, *The King James Only Controversy,* there is a similar chart in which he compares the KJV, NIV, and NASB. Of twelve primary references to Christ's deity, the NASB is clear in 10 of 12 Scriptures. The NIV does it one better, clearly teaching Christ's deity in 11 of 12 Scriptures. But, horrors, the KJV is clear on only 6 of 12 Scriptures.[43] Does all this seem like a conspiracy to deny the deity of Christ? If so, why did the new versions *correct* the KJV in order to properly *declare* the deity of Christ?

For example, in Titus 2:13 and 2 Peter 1:1, the KJV inaccurately translates these passages by splitting the terms "God" and "Saviour," thus distinguishing the person of God from the person of Jesus. They read "the great God *and our* Saviour, Jesus Christ." This rendering wrongly implies two persons are spoken of: 1) the great God, *and* 2) our Saviour Jesus Christ. Jehovah's Witnesses use this ambiguity to argue that Jesus Christ is not "the great God" but only "our savior." The King James translators translated the words this way because they were unaware of a grammatical rule of the Koine Greek—the Granville Sharp Rule—which was not discovered until the early nineteenth century.

According to Dr. Wallace, "the *King James* translators knew Greek less well than they knew Latin and so they constantly relied on the Latin to get themselves through the Greek."[44] This helps explain why the KJV mistranslates Titus 2:13, 2 Peter 1:1, and other places that clearly teach the deity of Christ. As noted, Greek grammarian Granville Sharp wrote a monograph in 1798 on the Greek construction of Titus 2:13, 2 Peter 1:1, etc., and formulated a rule which, despite claims to the contrary, has universally proven true in the New Testament. When defined properly, "*it is found to be entirely without exception.*"[45]

Regardless, in his day (200 years ago), some people were saying Sharp's argument was false and that these verses did not prove the deity of Christ. Like today, they were using the King James Bible in defense of their heresy of Arianism.[46]

The NIV, NASB, etc., have the proper translation at this point due to their knowledge of this rule. They render it: "Our great God *and* Savior, Jesus Christ"— showing that Jesus is both our God and our Savior.

The KJV also "denies" the deity of Christ in John 1:18 when it states, "No man hath seen God at any time; the only begotten *Son*, which is in the bosom of the Father, he hath declared him." The NIV translates it, "No one has ever seen God, but *God the One and Only*, who is at the Father's side, has made him known." The NASB translates, "No man has seen God at any time; *the only begotten God*, who is in the bosom of the Father, He has explained Him." The Greek term *theos* (God) "has the support of all the earliest manuscript papyri that we have, P66, P75."[47]

In light of this, should we argue that it is really the KJO supporters who are the ones endorsing a translation that denies Christ's deity? Of course not. This would be just as unfair as the KJO approach to the new translations. The deity of Christ is still clearly taught in other places in the KJV. But lacking the help of modern scholarship, the followers of the KJV are less prepared to defend such doctrines as the deity of Christ and salvation by grace at certain points than those who use modern, clearer translations.

Consider a final example. A key argument of KJO supporters in defense of the "satanic" nature of the new translations can supposedly be seen in how the new translations translate Isaiah 14:12. Here they allegedly mistranslate the person of Lucifer or Satan as the person of Jesus Christ. Obviously, making the Person of Christ become the person of Satan would be horrible blasphemy. But did this really happen? The KJV reads, "How art thou fallen from heaven, O Lucifer, son of the morning!" The NASB and NIV read, "How you have fallen from heaven, O star of the morning" (or "O morning star"), son of the dawn."

Why did the KJV use the term "Lucifer" and modern versions the term "morning star"? The term *Lucifer* came to us by way of Jerome's Latin Bible, the *Vulgate*, which the KJV translators sometimes used for their own translation. The Latin word for "morning star" *is* "Lucifer." This word was used to refer to Venus, the morning star, and was applied figuratively to the pride and fall of the king of Babylon.

Now, to associate the morning star with someone other than the king of Babylon is an interpretation which must be brought to this verse from somewhere else. So how did *Lucifer* (Latin for "morning star") become equated with the evil personage of Satan, the devil? This is something that the medieval Church authorities imported into this text, without direct scriptural warrant.[48] In other words, to associate the Latin word "the morning star"—*lucifer*—with the concept of the devil or Satan can only be suggested in a secondary sense.

Of course, we know that the true bright and morning star is Jesus because in Revelation 22:16 (KJV) Jesus says, "I am…the bright and morning star." But this does not mean that Isaiah can't use the Hebrew word for morning star to also speak of the king of Babylon.

In essence, the KJO writers may claim new translations have produced major doctrinal deviations from the faith, but this charge is entirely false. Anyone who wishes can examine any good English translation or any Greek text—whether the *Textus Receptus* (TR), *Majority Text* (MT), *Nestle-Aland*, NIV, KJV, NASB, RSV, NKJV, etc.—and guess what? They will derive the exact same doctrinal and ethical beliefs.

6

Were heretics, occultists, and homosexuals on the translation committees?

Proponents of the KJO often claim that unbelievers, heretics, occultists, and/or homosexuals have been members of the editorial or translation committees of the modern versions which biased their translation in favor of heresy, occultism, and sexual sin. This is another gross distortion.

Riplinger, for example, claims that lesbian sympathizer Virginia Mollencott was involved in the NIV translation.[49] It is true that Mollencott sat on the literary (stylistic) committee of the NIV, but only for a few months. However, she had nothing to do with the *translation*, and once her sexual views were known, she was asked to resign.[50] On "The John Ankerberg Show," Dr. Kenneth Barker, the NIV general editor, stated that no one was aware of Mollencott's sexual preference at the time. (The NIV was finished in 1978; Mollencott's sexual views were not known until 1983.) If the committee had known, "we would not have consulted her at all." Regardless, she "was consulted briefly and only in a minor way on matters of English style" and "she did not influence the NIV translators and editors in any of their final decisions. Not one."[51]

Further, the KJO people's claim that the NIV encourages sodomy through its translations is also completely false. In the words of Dr. Barker, "Homosexual and lesbian practices are condemned just as clearly and strongly in the NIV as in any other English version." (See Leviticus 18:22; 20:13; Romans 1:26,27; 1 Corinthians 6:9,10; 1 Timothy 1:10; and Jude 7.)

Consider another example: Riplinger cites alleged evidence to imply that Greek New Testament scholar B.F. Westcott was involved in spiritism and, therefore, his work should not be trusted.[52] (Westcott coproduced the 1881 edition of the Greek NT which set the pattern for almost all future editions of the Greek text.) Riplinger's allegations are false. For example, she confuses B.F. Westcott with the mortician-spiritualist W.W. Westcott, theorizing the latter individual was actually the former. Yet B.F. Westcott was born in 1825 while W.W. Westcott wasn't born until 1848.[53] Riplinger also cites Arthur Westcott, the son of B.F. Westcott, as supposedly confessing that his father *was* a spiritualist. In fact, he merely said that his father had seriously investigated spiritualism and concluded, just as seriously, that "such investigations led to no good."[54]

Concerning Westcott's beliefs, Dr. James Price, the former executive editor of the *New King James Version* Old Testament, commented in a personal letter to Ms. Riplinger:

> I just finished reading Westcott's commentary on Hebrews 1:1-3. He makes such strong, clear statements about the Word of God, the Trinity, the deity of Christ, the incarnation, and redemption that it is hard to doubt his orthodoxy on these doctrines. We may disagree with Westcott and Hort on some of their doctrinal views, but their doctrinal views had little to do with the development of their method of textual criticism, a scientific method for deciding which readings of the Greek New Testament are most likely original. It is wrong to make a connection between their doctrinal views and their scientific methodology. Present day scholars, who accept their method of textual criticism, accept it on the basis of its scientific merit, not because they agree with their theology.[55]

In conclusion, the charges of gross immorality or deliberate corruption related to the translation committees of modern godly versions are not only false, they are also slanderous. Solomon's wisdom was evident when he wrote, "a slanderer separates intimate friends" and, thus, "he who spreads slander is a fool" (NIV: Proverbs 16:28; 10:18; see also Ephesians 4:31).

7

Are modern versions less readable than the KJV?

Riplinger and other KJO proponents claim that scientific tests have been conducted which prove the readability of the KJV is equal or superior to that of modern translations—something that anyone who has ever read the KJV might find difficult to accept. Dr. Arthur Farstad, executive editor of *The New King James Version* New Testament, discussed this subject in his book *The New King James Version in the Great Tradition*. The test results obtained by the NKJV editors showed, as would be expected, that the KJV was *more* difficult to understand than modern translations. The KJV required a 12th grade reading level while the NASB, was at 11, the RSV 10.4, the TLB 8.3, the NKJV 8, and the NIV 7.8.[56]

Further, if the new versions are satanic, how could we find statements like that of the general editor of the NIV, Kenneth Barker, who comments, "My files are replete with testimonial letters from people all over the world testifying as to how they've been brought to Christ—a saving knowledge, a saving faith in Christ, through reading the NIV....Christians from all over the world...have been blessed and spiritually taught and matured in their Christian life through using the NIV."[57] Doesn't the fact that the KJV has sales of 350 million in 400 years but NIV sales were 100 million in just 15 years say something about readability?

Indeed the reading difficulty of the KJV w
primary impetus for the NKJV. It cannot be denied
that there are many places where the KJV is anything
but clear due to its 400-year-old language. Here are a
few examples of words and phrases from the KJV that
have passed completely out of use and convey no
meaning to readers today: "chambering" (Romans
13:13); "cieled" (Haggai 1:4); "clouted upon their feet"
(Joshua 9:5); "cotes" (2 Chronicles 32:28); "sureti-
ship" (Proverbs 11:15); "sackbut" (Daniel 3:5);
"scall" (Leviticus 13:30); "brigandines" (Jeremiah
46:4); "amerce" (Deuteronomy 22:19); "crookbackt"
(Leviticus 21:20); "glede" (Deuteronomy 14:13);
"wen" (Leviticus 22:22); "nitre" (Proverbs 25:20);
and "tabret" (Genesis 31:27).[58] In addition, we find
words like almug, neesing, chode, habergeon, purte-
nance, aceldama, blains, wot, trow, churl, ambassage,
collops of fat, wimples, hole's mouth, ouches of gold,
naughty figs, and fetched a compass (which does not
mean to go *find* a compass but "to turn around").
These were the words chosen by KJV translators in
their day to signify the meaning of the Hebrew and
Greek words. But who understands the meaning of
such old English terms today? Translators now find
current English words in use that more accurately
convey the meaning for our own era.

8

What have Bible scholars and other researchers concluded about the arguments and methodology in Riplinger's *New Age Bible Versions?*

G.A. Riplinger's book *New Age Bible Versions* (A.V.
Publications, 1993) has caused a great deal of controversy among Christian laypeople and even pastors. On
the back cover of Riplinger's book we read:

> This book is a result of an exhaustive six year colla-
> tion of *new* bible versions, their underlying Greek
> manuscripts, editions, and editors. It *objectively* and
> methodologically documents the *hidden* alliance between
> *new* versions and the New Age Movement's One World
> Religion....The Greek manuscripts, critical editions,
> lexicons and dictionaries behind the *new* versions are
> examined, revealing their *occult origins*, contents, and
> yet unreleased material—a *blueprint for the Antichrist's
> One World Religion and Government*....Each page opens
> a door exposing new version editors *in agreement with
> Luciferians, occultists, and New Age philosophy* in mental
> institutions, seance parlors, prison cells, and courtrooms
> for heresy trials and most shocking of all *denying that sal-
> vation is through faith in Jesus Christ*....Documented are
> the thousands of words, verses, and doctrines by which
> new versions will prepare the apostate churches of these
> last days *to accept the religion of the Antichrist* even his
> mark, image and Lucifer worship. [Emphasis added.]

Riplinger has stated publicly that she receives direct
revelations from God.[59] Concerning *New Age Bible
Versions (NABV)* she further wrote that she received
daily divine guidance—so much so that the book was
primarily authored by God: "Daily, during the six years
needed for this investigation [to write the book], the
Lord miraculously brought the needed materials and
resources—much like the ravens fed Elijah. Each discovery was *not the result of effort on my part, but of the
direct hand of God*—so much so that I hesitated to even
put my name on the book. Consequently, I used G.A.
Riplinger, which signifies to me, God and Riplinger—
God as author and Riplinger as secretary."[60]

Even KJO promoter David W. Cloud refers to this
statement as "amazing and frightful."[61] If, in Riplinger's
opinion, God is the primary author of her book, then
it must constitute divine revelation. It must therefore
be inerrant and, consequently, uncorrectable.

To claim that God is the very author of your book
when it has literally hundreds of errors—and yet maintain at the same time that one is attempting to safe-
guard the *character* of God by defending the *inerrancy*
of the KJV—is a bit difficult to argue. Yet Dr. Joseph
R. Chambers, a promoter of Gail Riplinger, claims, "I

can assure you, every documentation that I have researched of Gail Riplinger, I have found it to be accurate and I have found it to be absolutely clear."[62]

NABV will not be the last KJO book and it certainly wasn't the first. But it is characteristic of the genre, and a classic example of how not to write a book. Although some people, like Texe Marrs, have hailed her book ("It may be the most important book ever written"), the general consensus of evangelical scholars is that it, like other KJO literature generally, is so seriously flawed as to be virtually worthless. Here are what some scholars have said regarding *NABV*.[63] (Note 63 provides documentation for the following quotations.)

James White calls *NABV* "a study in misrepresentation" and comments: "Riplinger's information is fatally flawed and utterly untrustworthy"; "I have only once or twice encountered a work that contained more misrepresentation of historical facts, of cited sources of documentation, and of the writings of those who are being reviewed"; "the modern versions are unashamedly misrepresented in place after place by the convenient use of punctuation.... Double standards are rampant throughout the book."

Dr. Don Wilkins, a translator on the NASB, comments generally concerning the alleged evidence and documentation cited in Riplinger's book, "I think it's ridiculous, it's careless, it's full of holes. Everything I've seen in Riplinger's book, virtually everything she says is either a misquotation or a misleading of the truth." (The NASB Editorial Board of the Lockman Foundation also spent six weeks investigating Riplinger's allegations and found them entirely false.[64])

H. Wayne House, professor at large at Simon Greenleaf University, author and lecturer who holds earned doctorates in both theology and law as well as a master's degree in biblical and patristic Greek, comments, "The foolishness of its various claims are transparent when one takes the time to study them....*NABV* is replete with logical, philosophical, theological, biblical, and technical errors....Riplinger incessantly quotes people out of context....[She] does this repeatedly, page after page...."

Dr. Robert Morey remarks, "This is beyond all doubt the worst book I have ever read. Its pages bristle with so many logical fallacies and biblical, theological, historical and linguistic errors that one wonders where to start."

Doug Kutilek comments, "…factual errors…dwell on page-after-page of her book. She misuses terms, misrepresents manuscript evidence, exaggerates evidence that seems to support her view, suppresses that which contradicts it, repeatedly abuses Scripture and contorts its meaning, employs defective logic, repeatedly fails to document evidence, displays gross ignorance of both Greek and Hebrew, selectively applies criticisms to the NASB/NIV that equally apply to the KJV, and everywhere relies on unreliable authors for information."

Supporters of Ms. Riplinger would argue (irrelevantly) that such statements are made by those who are not KJO supporters. But even David W. Cloud, a staunch defender of the KJV, says the following of Riplinger's book:

> It is the *frequent error* in documentation, in logic, and in statement of fact that gives cause for alarm.…There are many good points made in the book, but *it is so marred by error, carelessness, and faulty logic that it cannot be used as a dependable resource*.…the documentation is *extremely unreliable*. A great many references that I attempted to check were not accurate. …*New Age Bible Versions*, from beginning to end, advances faulty logic. Mrs. Riplinger continually makes unequal and unfair comparisons and makes connections where no proper connections exist.…*New Age Bible Versions* contains countless statements which are entirely unsubstantiated.…

To illustrate Riplinger's approach, consider two examples. First, she is critical of the New King James Version (NKJV), claiming it is just as biased and error ridden as modern versions. She makes these claims even though the NKJV is based on the very *same* manuscripts as the KJV. Those who worked on the NKJV are appalled at her charges. For instance, Dr. James D. Price, the executive editor of the NKJV Old

Testament, in a personal letter to Riplinger (later published by *Baptist Biblical Heritage*), stated:

> As former Executive Editor of the New King James Version Old Testament, I have first-hand knowledge of the facts concerning the NKJV, the people who worked on it, the reasons why certain changes were made and the wording of the old King James Version, and the reasons why it was decided to produce the new version in the first place. This information is not secret, as you have stated, but has been made public in many promotional brochures produced by the publishers and in a book written by Dr. Arthur Farstad....I have read carefully what you have published about the NKJV, and am greatly concerned because everything you wrote about the NKJV is either false or inaccurate. (Used by permission, copy on file.)

In his letter, Dr. Price cited numerous illustrations of Riplinger's errors regarding the NKJV. For example, Riplinger claimed, "The NKJV and all new versions have abandoned the traditional Old Testament Hebrew Ben Chayyim Masoretic Text, and followed Rudolph Kittle's 1937 corruption of Biblia Hebraica Leningrad Ms B19a." As Price points out, the NKJV followed the Masoretic text, not Kittle's. Further, Kittle did not corrupt the Biblia Hebraica Leningrad Ms B19a; it is widely regarded as "perhaps the most faithful copy of the Masoretic Text, the Textus Receptus of the Hebrew Bible." In fact, "as former executive editor of the NKJV Old Testament, I can confidently assure you that the NKJV followed, as carefully as possible...the Bobmerg 1524–25 Ben Chayyim edition that the KJV 1611 translators used—I personally made sure."

Unfortunately, Riplinger's treatment of the NKJV is characteristic of her treatment of the NIV and NASB as well.

To illustrate, on page 455 of Riplinger's text, she claims that the NASB has deleted "the key words, 'on Thee.'" She cites the NASB of Isaiah 26:3 as follows, "The steadfast of mind Thou wilt keep in perfect peace." Alongside it, she cites the KJV, "Thou wilt keep him in perfect peace, whose mind is stayed on Thee." But Riplinger's argument that the NASB has deleted these key words is false. Riplinger's comparison is as follows:

Isaiah 26:3

NASB	KJV
The steadfast of mind Thou wilt keep in perfect peace.	Thou wilt keep him in perfect peace, whose mind is stayed on thee.

Riplinger has distorted what both the NASB and KJV state. All one has to do is compare the verses. Here is what the NASB and KJV actually state:

Isaiah 26:3

NASB	KJV
The steadfast of mind Thou wilt keep in perfect peace, Because he trusts in Thee.	Thou wilt keep *him* in perfect peace, *whose* mind *is* stayed *on Thee*: because he trusteth in thee.

Clearly, Riplinger has claimed that key words are missing when they are not. Also, Riplinger's quotation of the KJV does *not* place the words "on thee" (or "him," "whose," "is") in italics. The King James translators italicized these words so the reader would understand that the words were not in the original Hebrew but were added for readability. Thus Riplinger has claimed "key words" were deleted that never were *in* the Bible to begin with.

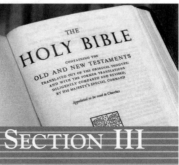

SECTION III

Ancient
Manuscript
Evidence, Bible
Translations, and
Biblical Inerrancy

9

What about the preservation and classification of the ancient manuscripts?

Today more than 5300 Greek manuscripts (mss.) or mss. portions exist. Since there is no 100 percent perfect manuscript, scholars examine all the evidence from all the mss. and weigh them accordingly. It is this examination of all the data that has proven that we not only have 100 percent of the autographs but that we have also established the original text at a 98-99 percent certainty. *All* translations translate the *same* Greek text over 98 percent of the time.

As noted, the number of variants that are of any significance is small.[65] (Note 65 documents the following information.) The premiere American Greek scholar, Dr. A.T. Robertson, who is familiar with the most minute details of the Greek text, estimated that the textual variants amounted to only "a thousandth part of the entire text." Westcott and Hort estimated the New Testament text was "98.33 percent pure whether or not one used the *Textus Receptus* or their own Greek text." Noted church historian Philip Schaff estimated there were only 400 variants that affected the sense of a passage, and only 50 were actually important—but none affecting an article of faith or preceptive duty. Dr. Gorden Fee points out that, for most scholars, over 90 percent of the variants are resolved.

Dr. Rene Pache remarks of the great Princeton scholar B.B. Warfield that he declared "that the great bulk of the New Testament has been transmitted to us without, or almost without, any variations. It can be asserted with confidence that the sacred text is exact and valid and that no article of faith and no moral precept in it has been distorted or lost."

The same is true for the Old Testament. William Green, Hebrew grammarian and professor of Hebrew, Biblical, and Oriental Literature at Princeton Seminary, makes a similar statement relating to the Old

Testament and observes that no other work of antiquity has been so accurately preserved.

Eminent Old Testament scholar Dr. Robert Dick Wilson agreed. After 30 years of exceptionally thorough research, using the laws of legal evidence, involving investigation of every consonant in the entire Old Testament (some 1¼ million), including manuscript variations, Wilson concluded, "I can affirm that there is not a page of the Old Testament concerning which we need have any doubt" and, apart from minor copyists mistakes, "We can be absolutely certain" that "we have the text of the Old Testament that Christ and the Apostles had, and which was in existence from the beginning."

Among the variants that do exist, textual critics seek to determine the *original* reading. In order to help do this, they have catalogued the mss. into basic geographical "families" or text types which share certain characteristics and/or common readings that separate them from other manuscripts. The three basic families are the Alexandrian (from Egypt), the Western (Roman), and the Byzantine (from Constantinople). Generally, the Alexandrian family contains the fewest and earliest manuscripts whereas the Byzantine contains the later and great majority of manuscripts. How did this come about?

We know that the apostles wrote and sent their letters to different churches in different geographical regions in the Roman Empire. Christians began copying these letters in other languages for missionary purposes or to give to their family and friends. Soon copies were circulating in a large number of languages. As time went by, many of these copies began to accumulate in certain geographical areas and came to be referred to in groups. Thus, when the people in the Western part of the Roman Empire began to turn away from Greek and spoke primarily Latin, many of their New Testament documents were translated and copied in Latin. Both the Greek and Latin documents from this geographical area are called "The Western Text" family. Another family of manuscripts comes from the geographical area of Alexandria, Egypt, and is called

"The Alexandrian Text" family. The third family comes from the geographical area surrounding the city of Byzantium, later renamed Constantinople and known today as Istanbul, Turkey. Ninety percent of the manuscripts of the New Testament that have survived have come from this area and are known as "The Byzantine Family of Documents." Out of this family has also come what is known as the Majority Text, so named because it adopts readings on the basis of numerical majority. It is believed that the reading found in most mss. is probably the original.

But no one can, with 100 percent accuracy, prove that any given manuscript family or tradition is superior. Again, this does not present a problem. The differences between the majority of later mss. and the minority of earlier mss. are insignificant—surely a testimony to the accuracy of both traditions. The consensus of godly, conservative scholarship is that it does little good to assume without evidence that only the largest family of manuscripts has been preserved in order to produce one perfect Bible when we have much earlier evidence that must be weighed on the basis of the best criteria we have. This approach is known as an eclectic approach because it attempts to ascertain the most original reading from all the manuscript data. It would seem the eclectic approach is the best option since KJO writers cannot *prove* that the Majority Text is the most correct.

The error of those who defend the KJV only is that they assume there is only *one* family of manuscripts (the Byzantine or Majority Text) and one pure text (the KJV translation based on the TR) which are to act as the ultimate standard in deciding the proper variant readings from the thousands of Greek manuscripts and, thus, what is to become the best Bible.

Why do the vast majority of evangelical scholars accept the readings of the *minority* of earlier manuscripts rather than the readings of the *majority* of later manuscripts? Because the closer one proceeds to the original autographs, the less time exists for corruption. God has not told us which manuscript family is the closest to the original, and *no* Byzantine mss. exist before the fourth century, so King James proponents cannot claim *proof* of having the "best" Bible. They simply don't know. In other words, arguments for accepting the later or earlier mss. are based on assumptions. The issue is whose assumptions are more credible given the evidence at hand.[66]

Manuscripts must be weighed in terms of their overall value and not merely counted by number. All mss. and all internal and external evidence should be evaluated in order to rate variant readings in terms of degrees of certainty. This means that, in very rare and ultimately insignificant cases, we will never know with 100 percent accuracy the single proper reading. But we *will* know that the proper reading exists among the variants we possess.

Even Dr. Daniel B. Wallace, an expert on the ancient Greek texts and former 17-year Majority Text advocate, comments, "I've examined many of the best ancient manuscripts in the world firsthand and I've had a chance to spend hundreds of hours in this field and I have since switched my views to a more reasoned, eclectic view where I would agree with the text behind these modern translations."[67]

10

How are translations made?

Translating the entire Bible from Hebrew and Greek to another language is a very arduous, time-consuming endeavor requiring great skill and knowledge. Translators must not only be experts in at least three (usually more) languages, they must decide which translation approach to use. In what is termed "formal equivalency," a more literal "word for word" approach is adopted—as in the KJV, NASB, NKJV, etc. In what is termed "dynamic equivalency," translators will seek to sacrifice literalness to better translate the *meaning* of the Scripture, as in the NIV, LB, etc. The problem, of course, is that concern with *meaning* brings translators more into the realm of *interpretation* than strict translation and thus opens them to interpretive criticisms. However, a truly literal word-for-word translation would, at best, be awkward and difficult as can be seen in any Greek-English Interlinear.

Furthermore, all translation work of necessity involves some degree of interpretation. Even formal translations like the KJV and NASB must also contain some degree of dynamic equivalency. In Matthew 27:44 (KJV) it says the thieves on the cross, "cast the same in his teeth." But in the Greek the terms "cast," "same," "his," and "teeth" are not there. These words are a dynamic equivalent of "they reviled him."

The best approach is to find the overall balance between readability and accuracy. For example, while the NASB is more formal than the dynamic NIV, both are illustrative of seeking to blend readability and accuracy.

Anyone familiar with translation issues knows that there is more than one proper manner by which to translate many Greek and Hebrew words or phrases into English. Therefore, it is incorrect to argue that there is only *one* correct way to translate certain words. For example, in 2 Timothy 2:15 the Greek word *spoudazo* is translated as "be diligent" (NASB), "do your utmost" (MLB), "work hard" (TLB), "do your best" (NIV, RSV), and "study" (KJV). Notice that the last two translations, "do your best" and "study," do not carry quite the same force as the first three translations. In this case the Greek word is part of a family of terms whose primary emphasis is haste and speed, and by extension, zeal, earnestness, and eagerness, as well as carrying the idea of being at pains and "making every effort to accomplish something." Therefore, the NASB, MLB, and TLB are more expressive of the original, while the KJV, RSV, and NIV are less emphatic and tend to miss the force of the Greek term. This illustrates not only how translations may sometimes fail to carry the precise force of a Greek or Hebrew word, but also how one Greek word can be accurately translated in at least three different ways.[68]

In the differences one does find among good translations, there is characteristically a quite logical reason why the translators chose the word(s) they did, based on translation approach, accepted principles of translation, literary style, and so forth. Many illustrations are given in Kenneth Barker's *Accuracy Defined and Illustrated* (see Recommended Reading). A book such as his provides a great deal of insight into the translation process.

To sum up, the reason for differences among modern translations is due to the unavoidable aspects of the very nature of the translation process. But a quality translation is based on a great deal of godly scholarship, with every attempt made to ascertain the original rendering through examination of all the textual sources. The end product is a highly readable and useful translation which can be trusted.

11

If no translation is 100 percent perfect, how do we know we have an inerrant Bible?

In the last two decades, the topic of biblical inerrancy has separated the evangelical camp into those who are inerrantists and those who are not. Inerrantists believe "that when all facts are known, the Scriptures in their original autographs and properly interpreted will be shown to be wholly true in everything that they affirm, whether that has to do with doctrine or morality or with the social, physical, or life sciences."[69]

Those who reject inerrancy believe there are original errors in certain areas the Bible touches outside doctrine and morality, e.g., in science and history. But if Scripture contains errors in those areas we *can* test on the basis of historical, archaeological, and scientific fact, on what logical basis can we assume it doesn't contain errors in those areas we *cannot* test such as theology and ethics (the nature of God, salvation, morality)?

The truth is that no error can be proven in the autographs since we don't have them. In His wisdom, God has seen fit not to preserve them. The original God-breathed manuscripts would of certainty have become items of worship, and, as with the Koran of Islam, translations would likely have been prohibited or rejected as causing a "perverting" of the pure Word of God. This eventually might have kept Scripture from all but those studied in Greek and Hebrew.

Regardless, an error can't logically be suggested in the autographs because our copies strongly support inerrancy. Dr. Gleason L. Archer was an undergraduate classics major who received training in Latin, Greek, French, and German at Harvard University. At seminary he majored in Hebrew, Aramaic, and Arabic and in post-graduate study became involved with Akkadian and Syriac, teaching courses on these subjects. He has had a special interest in middle-kingdom Egyptian studies. At the Oriental Institute in Chicago he did specialized study in Eighteenth Dynasty historical records as well as studying Coptic and Sumerian. In addition, he obtained a full law degree and was admitted to the Massachusetts Bar. He has also visited the Holy Land where he inspected most of the important archeological sites and spent time in Beirut, Lebanon, for a specialized study of modern literary Arabic. He holds a B.D. from Princeton Theological Seminary and a Ph.D. from Harvard Graduate School.

This background enabled him to become expert in the issue of charges of alleged errors and contradictions in Scripture:

> In my opinion this charge can be refuted and its falsity exposed by an objective study done in a consistent, evangelical perspective....I candidly believe I have been confronted with just about all the biblical difficulties under discussion in theological circles today—especially those pertaining to the interpretation and defense of Scripture....As I have dealt with one apparent discrepancy after another and have studied the alleged contradictions between the biblical record and the evidence of linguistics, archeology, or science, my confidence in the trustworthiness of Scripture has been repeatedly verified and

strengthened by the discovery that almost every problem in Scripture that has ever been discovered by man, from ancient times until now, has been dealt with in a completely satisfactory manner by the biblical text itself—or else by objective archeological information.[70]

Given the fact that Dr. Archer has graduated from Princeton and Harvard, done extensive studies in archaeology and other areas, become fluent in 15 languages, received full training in legal evidences, etc., the above statement can hardly be summarily dismissed.

But there are many similar testimonies by other competent scholars. Dr. Robert Dick Wilson (Ph.D., Princeton), an Old Testament authority and author of *A Scientific Investigation of the Old Testament*, could read the New Testament in nine different languages by the age of 25. In addition, he could repeat from memory a Hebrew translation of the entire New Testament without missing a single syllable and do the same with large portions of the Old Testament. He proceeded to learn 45 languages and dialects and was also a master of paleography and philology: "I have made it an invariable habit never to accept an objection to a statement of the Old Testament without subjecting it to a most thorough investigation, linguistically and factually," and "I defy any man to make an attack upon the Old Testament on the grounds of evidence that I cannot investigate." His conclusion was that no critic has succeeded in proving an error in the Old Testament.[71]

Theologian, philosopher, and trial attorney John Warwick Montgomery, holding nine graduate degrees in different fields, observes, "I myself have never encountered an alleged contradiction in the Bible which could not be cleared up by the use of the original languages of the Scriptures and/or by the use of accepted principles of literary and historical interpretation."[72]

John W. Haley examined 900 alleged problems in Scripture and concluded, "I cannot but avow, as the [conclusion] of my investigation, the profound conviction that *every difficulty and discrepancy in the scriptures is...capable of a fair and reasonable solution.*"[73] Dr.

William Arndt concluded in his own study of alleged contradictions and errors in the Bible, "[W]e may say with full conviction that no instances of this sort occur anywhere in the Scriptures."[74]

Clearly the evidence lies in favor of biblical inerrancy. This is in harmony with what the Bible itself teaches.* If what God says is true by definition, note God's description of His own Word.

1. The Old Testament

Eternal: "The grass withers, the flower fades, but the word of our God stands forever" (Isaiah 40:8); "Forever, O LORD, Thy word is settled in heaven" (Psalm 119:89).

Perfect and trustworthy: "Every word of God is tested;...Do not add to His words, lest He reprove you, and you be proved a liar" (Proverbs 30:5,6); "The words of the LORD are pure words; as silver tried in a furnace on the earth, refined seven times" (Psalm 12:6).

True: "the word of truth"; "Thy law is truth"; "all Thy commandments are truth"; "the sum of Thy word is truth" (Psalm 119:43,142,151,160).

Holy and righteous: "For He remembered His holy word with Abraham His servant" (Psalm 105:42); "Thy righteous word" (Psalm 119:123); "Thy word is very pure, therefore Thy servant loves it" (Psalm 119:140).

Good: "I will fulfill the good word which I have spoken" (Jeremiah 33:14).

Vital (and verbal): "'And as for Me, this is My covenant with them,' says the LORD: 'My Spirit which is upon you, and My words which I have put in your mouth, shall not depart from your mouth, nor from the mouth of your offspring, nor from the mouth of your offspring's offspring,' says the LORD, 'from now and forever'" (Isaiah 59:21).

---

* Unless otherwise indicated, Scriptures in this section are from the NASB.

2. **The Gospels** (Jesus' view of God's Word)

Eternal: "Heaven and earth will pass away, but My words shall not pass away" (Matthew 24:35).

Trustworthy: "the Scripture cannot be broken" (John 10:35); "For I did not speak on My own initiative, but the Father Himself who sent Me has given Me commandment, what to say, and what to speak....Therefore the things I speak, I speak just as the Father has told me" (John 12:49,50); "But it is easier for heaven and earth to pass away than for one stroke of a letter of the Law to fail" (Luke 16:17).

True: "Sanctify them in the truth; Thy word is truth" (John 17:17).

Holy: "My teaching is not Mine, but His who sent Me" (John 7:16; see also 12:49,50).

Vital (and verbal): "But He answered and said, 'It is written, "MAN SHALL NOT LIVE ON BREAD ALONE, BUT ON EVERY WORD THAT PROCEEDS OUT OF THE MOUTH OF GOD"'" (Matthew 4:4).

3. **The Rest of the New Testament** (the inspired apostles' view of God's Word)

Eternal: "'But the word of the Lord abides forever.' And this is the word which was preached to you" (1 Peter 1:25).

Inspired: "All Scripture is inspired by God" (2 Timothy 3:16; see also 2 Peter 3:2,15,16); "no prophecy was ever made by an act of human will, but men moved by the Holy Spirit spoke from God" (2 Peter 1:21).

Living and imperishable: "For the word of God is living and active" (Hebrews 4:12; cf. Acts 7:38); "for you have been born again not of seed which is perishable but imperishable, that is, through the living and abiding word of God" (1 Peter 1:23).

True: "Be diligent to present yourself approved to God as a workman who does not need to be ashamed, handling accurately the word of truth" (2 Timothy 2:15).

Not human: "And for this reason we also constantly thank God that when you received from us the word of God's message, you accepted it not as the word of men, but for what it really is, the word of God, which also performs its work in you who believe" (1 Thessalonians 2:13); "he who rejects this [instruction] is not rejecting man but the God who gives His Holy Spirit to you" (1 Thessalonians 4:8).

Holy: "from childhood you have known the sacred writings" (2 Timothy 3:15).

Vital (and verbal): "All Scripture is...profitable for teaching, for reproof, for correction, for training in righteousness; that the man of God may be adequate, equipped for every good work" (2 Timothy 3:16,17); "I testify to everyone who hears the words of the prophecy of this book: if anyone adds to them, God shall add to him the plagues which are written in this book; and if anyone takes away from the words of the book of this prophecy, God shall take away his part from the tree of life and from the holy city, which are written in this book" (Revelation 22:18,19); "Now we have received, not the spirit of the world, but the Spirit who is from God, that we might know the things freely given to us by God...[in words] taught by the Spirit" (1 Corinthians 2:12,13); "they have been entrusted with the very words (Greek: *logia*) of God" (Romans 3:2, NIV).

Although a great deal could be said about each of the above Scriptures (and there are many others), let us simply ask some questions. What did God mean when He called His word perfect, true, holy, righteous, good, trustworthy, and pure? Is perfection really imperfection? or truth really error? or good really something not good? or the trustworthy the doubtful? or the pure impure? Is it proper to call *errant* writings holy? How is inspiration *divine* if it merely guarantees the presence of truth and error? If God's Word is eternal, is it possible for the church to be content with a certain amount of *eternal* error? Dr. E.J. Young observes,

God has revealed to us His Word. What are we to think of Him if this Word is glutted with little annoying inaccuracies? ... He, of course, tells us that His Word is pure. If there are mistakes in that Word, however, we know better; it is not pure. If the autographa of Scripture are marred by flecks of mistake, God simply has not told us the truth concerning His Word. To assume that He could breathe forth a Word that contained mistakes is to say, in effect, that God Himself can make mistakes. We must maintain that the original of Scripture is infallible for the simple reason that it came to us directly from God Himself.[75]

Charles Spurgeon once wrote of the rudeness of those who question the inerrancy of God's Word when he stated, "This is the book untainted by any error, but is pure, unalloyed, perfect truth. Why? Because God wrote it. Ah! charge God with error if you please; tell *Him* that His book is not what it ought to be."[76]

Christians are to accept the teachings of Jesus because He is their Lord and Savior. But Jesus Himself never expressed any doubts about Scripture—at any time, in any manner. To the contrary, He accepted Scripture as God's inerrant word. Indeed, the strength of the case for a strict view of inerrancy can only be properly understood by a detailed study of Jesus' absolute trust in and use of Scripture.[77] For us, this alone is proof of scriptural inerrancy.

The weight of Jesus' words is impressive when we consider what they teach in more detail. In Matthew 5:17-19, e.g.,

The jot [KJV] is the smallest letter of the Hebrew alphabet and the tittle [KJV] is the minute horn or projection that distinguishes consonants of similar form from one another. It would be impossible to think of any expression that would bespeak the thought of the meticulous more adequately than precisely this one used here by our Lord.[78]

In John 10:35, e.g.,

[W]hen he says the Scripture cannot be broken, he is surely using the word Scripture in its most comprehensive denotation as including all that the Jews of the day recognized as Scripture, to wit, all the canonical books of the Old Testament. It is of the Old Testament

without any reservation or exception that he says it
cannot be broken. He affirms the unbreakableness of the
Scripture in its entirety and leaves no room for any such
supposition as that of degrees of inspiration and falli-
bility. Scripture is inviolable. Nothing less than this is
the testimony of our Lord.[79]

If it is easier for heaven and earth (i.e., the universe) to pass from existence than for the least stroke
of a pen to be lost, can we possibly believe Jesus
thought there were genuine errors in Scripture? And
if Jesus, God incarnate, said, "Thy word is truth," how
can Christians think otherwise? Montgomery
observes, "The weight of Christ's testimony to Scripture is so much more powerful than any alleged contradiction or error in the text or any combination of
them, that the latter must be adjusted to the former,
not the reverse."[80]

Dr. Montgomery comments on another statement
by Jesus found in Matthew 4:4 (KJV). Christ tells us
simply, quoting the God of the Old Testament, that
"'Man shall not live by bread alone, but by every word
that proceedeth out of the mouth of God.' One must
therefore operate with every word and consider every
word as significant. Had God intended otherwise, the
text would (by definition) be different from what it is!"[81]

Finally, the character of God Himself proves the
inerrancy of Scripture:

1. *Sovereign:* A sovereign God is able to preserve
   the process of inspiration from error.

2. *Righteousness:* A righteous God is unable to
   inspire error.

3. *Just:* A just God could not be untruthful in
   asserting His word is inerrant. He would be
   unjust if He bore witness to errant Scripture as
   holy and true.

4. *Love:* A loving God would adequately provide
   for the spiritual health and safety of His people
   by inspiring an inerrant Word.

5. *Eternal:* An eternal God has had forever to determine the canon and means of inspiration (e.g.,
   verbal, plenary) for His Word.

6. *Omniscient:* An omniscient God knows every contingency that might arise to inhibit inerrancy.

7. *Omnipotent:* An omnipotent God can effectively respond to every contingency and also preserve the transmission of His Word.

8. *Omnipresent:* An omnipresent God can initially reveal and inspire His Word and later illuminate it.

9. *Immutable:* An immutable God could never change His Word.

10. *Veracity:* A truthful God would not lie when He testifies about the inerrancy of His Word.

11. *Merciful:* A merciful God would not be unmerciful in inspiring both truth and error and then having His people vainly attempt to find the parts that are true. He would not leave His people to such subjectivism and uncertainty.

12. *Personal:* A personal God can inspire verbally, with words, to insure effective communication.

We close by citing the appropriate words of Dr. Paul Feinberg:

> I have never been able to understand how one can be justified in claiming absolute authority for the Scriptures and at the same time deny their inerrancy. This seems to be the height of epistemological nonsense and confusion. Let me try to illustrate the point. Suppose that I have an Amtrak railroad schedule. In describing its use to you, I tell you that it is filled with numerous errors but that it is absolutely authoritative and trustworthy.[82]

12

How does Romans 8:28 relate to the issues of modern translations?

Are modern translations really a curse upon the church? To the contrary, they are an obvious godsend. First, they have brought the Word of God to *hundreds of millions* of people who would not have had it otherwise and, in the process, made it easier to understand. Second, the greater the number of quality translations, the easier it is to understand the meaning of certain verses that may not be clear in any single translation. Thus, if we compare a NKJV, NIV, and NAS we will have three excellent translations that will give us the best attempts to ascertain the meaning of a particular passage that is unclear in one version.

Nor are the large number of manuscripts from different regions (the underlying basis for the dispute between the KJV and modern versions) any real problem for the church. They are really a blessing. That there are so many manuscripts from so many different places around the world has actually protected the integrity of the text. As White points out, if only one group of people had had access to the originals, or copies of the originals, we could never prove if that one group of people had decided at some point to change the text in order to conform to unbiblical church tradition or false doctrines. Thus, if any one group had complete control of the Bible, they would have the ability to manipulate it to their own ends. The vast number of manuscripts around the world make this an impossibility.[83] It is easy to see the wisdom of divine providence behind this. In exchange for the incalculable benefits of having the Scriptures disseminated around the world and of preserving the text and preventing its corruption, the overall cost is a whopping one or two percent of minor textual variants.

In an important class project, Dr. Daniel Wallace illustrates the preservation of the Bible by an exercise he has done over 35 times with his students. He takes an ancient apocryphal work and tells one student to change such and such for theological reasons and another student, because they are in a great hurry, to skip a few words, etc. The original manuscript is then discarded. What remains are 20 manuscripts, several generations removed from the original. "None of them at all look like each other, and the students say, 'There's no way we're going to get back to the original.' The nice thing is, I have the original. So when they work on this process [of attempting to ascertain the original text] through the normal means of textual criticism…they have come back to that original wording *every single time within one word.* And that one word that is missing is either 'also' or 'to.'"[84]

In other words, if a group of students can arrive at the original text within a single word how much more should Christians, with the wealth of mss. data they have, be assured that they have the original text?

In the end, the truth of Romans 8:28 will remain. Just as the unforeseen benefit of heresy in church history has been a spur to the church to formulate its doctrines and beliefs accurately, so the end result of divisions like the KJO controversy will be to spur Christians who love God to a fair and honest study of the issues. This will result in an understanding of God's Word that honors God, upholds the trustworthiness of Scripture, and recognizes the importance of the facts surrounding the origin and inspiration, text, transmission and translation of the Bible.

13

How should individual pastors and churches respond to the issue of new translations?

Hebrew 13:7,17 has instructions for both the leadership of the church and the church membership: "Remember your leaders, who spoke the word of God to you. Consider the outcome of their way of life and imitate their faith.…Obey your leaders and submit to their authority. They keep watch over you as men who must give an account. Obey them so that their work will be a joy, not a burden, for that would be of no advantage to you" (NIV).

These verses tell pastors and church leaders that they will give an account to God for how they have done their work as shepherds of God's flock. On the other hand, God tells His people to obey those in spiritual authority over them so that their task may be joyful rather than difficult. The Scripture also warns us to avoid those who cause dissensions and take note of them: "I urge you, brothers, to watch out for those who cause divisions....Keep away from them. For such people are not serving our Lord Christ" (Romans 16:17,18, NIV).

First, it should be recognized that the KJO issue is an unnecessary division that has caused significant problems for the church. "The KJV Only controversy is, in reality, a non-issue when compared with the serious challenges that face the Christian Church today. That so much time and effort has to be put into debunking the wild allegations of such individuals as Gail Riplinger is more of an indication of how easily American Christianity is distracted from its true purpose than anything else."[85]

Damage is done to the church in other ways: "The KJV Only position is forced to make statements about the Bible that in reality undercut the very foundations of the [Christian] faith....The willingness of many to sacrifice all semblance of logic and rationality in the cause of defending a great, yet imperfect, translation of the Bible as if it were in fact inspired, is used by skeptics as evidence of how 'backwards' conservatives *as a whole* truly are."[86]

Second, it would seem best for each individual church to make an official decision concerning a preferred translation. That translation can then be used for teaching, public reading, Scripture memorization, preaching, etc. Individuals, of course, would be free to use any translation they choose for personal study, but at least they will know that there is one specific translation used for church services.

Thus, if a given church is convinced that the Textus Receptus, the text behind the KJV, is the correct Greek text, then the KJV can be used. Better yet, preference for the NKJV should be considered since it is easier to understand. If a congregation accepts that the Majority Text is the best text for the New Testament then the NKJV should be adopted because it is the closest there is to the MT. Those churches who believe in an eclectic text, in examining all the evidence and making reasoned decisions on that basis, can use a good modern translation: Those who prefer a more word-for-word literal translation could use the NASB; those who want an easier version to read yet one that is still faithful could use the NIV.[87]

If church leadership exercises its God-given authority in a loving and proper manner, there should be no basis for this issue to become divisive in any church. And certainly, this is not an issue any Christian should break fellowship over.

CONCLUSION

Let's Be Grateful
for What We Do Have

Both KJO promoters and those who use modern translations have been more than blessed by God as far as His Word is concerned. They are privileged to have the Word of God more complete than the vast majority of God's people throughout history. Abraham and his family did not have the Word of God at all. Moses and the early Israelites had only the first few books of the Bible (the Pentateuch). King David had less than half the Old Testament. Even the apostle Paul had only the Old Testament. Early Christians to the fourth century had only the relatively few copies that were made and circulated in their particular locale. Christians from the fourth through sixteenth centuries had to be content with those few versions that existed prior to the King James—which were usually not even produced in their own language. Christians from the seventeenth to the nineteenth centuries had only the King James Version and a few others. And, until the use of the printing press became widespread the vast majority of believers couldn't even *own* a Bible. Copies were simply too expensive—even if they were available. Christians had to rely upon what was heard at church services.

By comparison, Christians of today are immeasurably richer—not only to have the King James translation, but to also have reliable modern versions. All believers should give thanks for the great wealth they do have rather than bickering over relatively minor differences among translations.

If you are a Christian who uses the King James Version—if you understand what you read and are comfortable with it—then by all means continue to use it. If you are a Christian who uses a good modern translation, you should also feel free to continue to use it. Don't be deterred or intimidated by those who would tell you that you do not have the true Word of God in your hands.

RECOMMENDED READING

"The John Ankerberg Show," transcript: "Which English Translation of the Bible Is Best for Christians to Use Today?" available from Ankerberg Theological Research Institute, P.O. Box 8977, Chattanooga, TN 37414.

James R. White. *The King James Only Controversy: Can You Trust the Modern Translations?* Bethany House Publishers, 1995.

D.A. Carson. *The King James Version Debate: A Plea for Realism.* Grand Rapids, MI: Baker Book House, 1979.

Kenneth Barker. *The NIV: The Making of a Contemporary Translation.* New York: International Bible Society, 1991.

Kenneth Barker. *Accuracy Defined and Illustrated.* Colorado Springs: International Bible Society, 1995.

Gustavus Paine. *The Men Behind the King James Version.* Grand Rapids, MI: Baker Book House, 1977.

Arthur L. Farstad. *The New King James Version in the Great Tradition.* Nashville: Thomas Nelson Publishers, 1993.

Norman Geisler and William E. Nix. *A General Introduction to the Bible.* Chicago: Moody Press, 1986, rev.

Moises Silva. *Biblical Words and Their Meaning: An Introduction to Lexical Semantics.* Grand Rapids, MI: Academie Books, 1983.

Jack P. Lewis. *The English Bible from KJV to NIV: A History and Evaluation.* Grand Rapids, MI: Baker Book House, 1984.

NOTES

1. Citations taken from Frank S. Meade, *The Encyclopedia of Religious Quotations*; Rhoda Tripp, *The International Thesaurus of Quotations*; Ralph L. Woods, *The World Treasury of Religious Quotations*; Jonathan Green, *Morrow's International Dictionary of Contemporary Quotations*.

2. Edwin A. Blum, "The Apostles' View of Scripture," in Norman Geisler, ed., *Inerrancy* (Grand Rapids: Zondervan Publishers, 1980), 49.

3. James R. White, *The King James Only Controversy* (Minneapolis: Bethany House Publishers, 1995), 40.

4. The Vedas are contradictory and incapable of uniform, objective interpretation. The Koran has also been corrupted (see John Ankerberg, John Weldon, *The Facts on Islam*). The texts and authenticity of the Buddhist canon is in doubt (John Weldon, "Buddhism and Nichren Shoshu Buddhism: A Critique," M.A. thesis, Simon Greenleaf University, 1987). Non-Judeo-Christian religious scriptures are either uncertain, corrupted, or incapable of logically and credibly verifying their claim to divine inspiration.

5. James R. White, prepublication manuscript, iii.

6. D.A. Carson, *The King James Version Debate: A Plea for Realism* (Grand Rapids, MI: Baker Book House, 1979), 73, second emphasis in original.

7. Illustrations taken from White, *King James Only Controversy*, 22, 132-33.

8. Ibid., 133.

9. Jack P. Lewis, *The English Bible from KJV to NIV: A History and Evaluation* (Grand Rapids, MI: Baker Book House, 1984), 38-39.

10. White, *King James Only Controversy*, 81; Lewis, *The English Bible*, 37-38.

11. Lewis, *The English Bible*, 39.

12. Norman Geisler, William Nix, *A General Introduction to the Bible* (Chicago: Moody Press, 1971), 384; the Metzger citation is also on this page.

13. Lewis, *The English Bible*, 39.

14. In Arthur L. Farstad, *The New King James Version in the Great Tradition* (Nashville: Thomas Nelson Publishers, 1989), 24.

15. Ibid., 111.

16. "The John Ankerberg Show," transcript, "Which English Translation of the Bible Is Best for Christians to Use Today?" 27. (All future references given as "Transcript.") See also White, *King James Only Controversy*, 6.

17. Transcript, 10,11.

18. White, *King James Only Controversy*, 224-28.

19. Ibid., 229.

20. Ibid., 231.

21. Lewis, *The English Bible*, 44-49.

22. White, *King James Only Controversy*, 231.

23. Ibid., 233.

24. Ibid., 237.

25. Lewis, *The English Bible*, 46-47.

26. Ibid.

27. Doug Kutilek, "The Septuagint: Riplinger's Blunders: Believe It or Not," *Baptist Biblical Heritage*, 5:2 (1994), 3.

28. Carson, *King James Version Debate*, 43.

29. Edited letter dated September 1, 1994.

30. Frank Logsdon, "From the NASV to the KJV," *O Timothy*, 9:1 (1992), 6; 11:8 (1994), 2.

31. Cited in White, *King James Only Controversy*, 95-109.

32. G.A. Riplinger, *New Age Bible Versions*, 1st. ed. (Munroe Falls, OH: A.V. Publications, 1993), 253.

33. White, *King James Only Controversy*, 146.

34. Riplinger, *New Age Bible Versions*, 498.

35. Ibid., 143.

36. Ibid., 145.

37. W.E. Vine's *An Expository Dictionary of New Testament Words* (Old Tappan, NJ: Revell Publishers, 1966), 1046; or Spiros Zodhiates' *The Complete Word Study Dictionary: New Testament* (1994), 1103.

38. G.A. Riplinger, "Why I Wrote the Book: *New Age Bible Versions*," *The End Times and Victorious Living*, Jan./Feb. 1994, 7, second emphasis added.

39. Cecil J. Carter, *The New American Standard Version and the Deity of Christ* (Lubbock, TX: Tabernacle Baptist Church), nd., tract B-29, 1.

40. Riplinger, *New Age Bible Versions*, 369.

41. Ibid., 306.

42. Carson, *King James Version Debate*, p. 64.

43. White, *King James Only Controversy*, 197.

44. Transcript, 29.

45. White, *King James Only Controversy*, 270.

46. Transcript, 29.

47. James White in Transcript, 31.

48. C.F. Keil, F. Delitzch, *Commentary on the Old Testament: Isaiah* (Grand Rapids, MI: Eerdmans, 1978), vol. 7, 311-12.

49. Cited in White, *New Age Bible Versions Refuted* (Phoenix: Alpha and Omega Ministries, 1994), 14.

50. Ibid., 14-15.

51. Transcript, 34.

52. Riplinger, *New Age Bible Versions*, 404-12.

53. White, *New Age Bible Versions Refuted*, 28; also James D. Price, letter to Gail Riplinger (undated; copy on file), 18ff.

54. Riplinger, *New Age Bible Versions*, 407; White, *New Age Bible Versions Refuted*, 28-29. Whether this was meant in a parapsychological or biblical context could not be determined by the secondary reference.

55. James D. Price, letter to Gail Riplinger (undated; copy on file), used with permission, 18.

56. Farstad, *New King James Version*, 4; cf., Price, letter, 55; White, prepublication manuscript, 219.

57. Transcript, 10.

58. White, *King James Only Controversy*, 236-37.

59. E.g., see White, *New Age Bible Versions Refuted*, 14.

60. Riplinger, "Why I Wrote the Book," 15, emphasis added.

61. David W. Cloud, "The Problem with *New Age Bible Versions*," *O Timothy*, vol. 11, is. 8 (1994), 11.

62. Transcript, 18.

63. The following quotations are taken from: White: *The King James Only Controversy*, 95; *New Age Bible Versions Refuted*, 1, 4, 7-8; Wilkins: Transcript, 17; H. Wayne House: "A Summary Critique: *New Age Bible Versions*," *Christian Research Journal*, Fall 1994, 46-48; Robert A. Morey: Book Review, *The Researcher*, Jan./Feb. 1994, 6; Doug Kutilek: "The Septuagint—Riplinger's Blunders: Believe It or Not," 12; Cloud: "The Problem with *New Age Bible Versions*," 2, 3, 6, 8, 10.

64. See "The View from Marrs," *Ankerberg Theological Research Institute News Magazine*, Nov. 1995, 16.

65. Primary documentation for the Westcott and Hort, Schaff and Robertson quotes is found in Norman Geisler and William Nix, *A General Introduction to the Bible*, 1st ed., 35, 238-39, 358, 365-67; and in Josh McDowell, *Evidence that Demands a Verdict* (San Bernardino, CA: Campus Crusade for Christ, 1972), 43-45. Fee is from White, *King James Only Controversy*, 39-40. Pache is from Rene Pache, *The Inspiration and Authority of Scripture* (Chicago: Moody Press, 1969), 193, citing Benjamin B. Warfield, *An Introduction to the Textual Criticism of the Old Testament*, 12 ff.; and "The Greek Testament of Westcott and Hort," *The Presbyterian Review*, vol. 3 (April 1882), 356. Green is from William Henry Green, *General Introduction to the Old Testament—The Text* (New York: Scribner's Sons, 1899), 181. The Wilson quote and data are from R.D. Wilson, "What Is an Expert?" lecture published in *Bible League Quarterly*, 1959, as given in David Otis Fuller, ed., *Which Bible?* 2d ed. (Grand Rapids, MI: Grand Rapids International Publications, rev. 1971), 44-45.

66. A few balanced, scholarly proponents for the *general* superiority of the KJV family have provided a necessary corrective in balancing what had become an overdependence on only one spectrum of NT manuscript evidence. White, *King James Only Controversy*, 5-6; Farstad, *New King James Version*, 107-10; cf. Zane Hodges and Arthur Farstad, *The Greek New Testament According to the Majority Text* (Nashville: Nelson, 1985).

67. Transcript, 38.

68. White, *King James Only Controversy*, 140.

69. Paul D. Feinberg, "The Meaning of Inerrancy" in Norman L. Geisler, ed., *Inerrancy* (Grand Rapids, MI: Zondervan Publishers, 1980), 294.

70. Gleason Archer, *Encyclopedia of Bible Difficulties* (Grand Rapids, MI: Zondervan Publishers, 1982), 11-12.

71. R.D. Wilson, *A Scientific Investigation of the Old Testament*, 13, 20, 130, 162-63; David Otis Fuller ed., *Which Bible?* (Grand Rapids, MI: Grand Rapids International Publications, rev. 1971), 44.

72. John Warwick Montgomery, *The Shape of the Past* (Minneapolis: Bethany, 1975), 176.

73. John W. Haley, *Alleged Discrepancies of the Bible* (Grand Rapids, MI: Baker Book House, 1982), rpt., vii.

74. William Arndt, *Does the Bible Contradict Itself?* (St. Louis: Concordia, 1955), rpt., XI.

75. Edward J. Young, *Thy Word Is Truth* (Grand Rapids, MI: Eerdmans, 1970), 86-87.

76. In Harold Lindsell, *The Battle for the Bible* (Grand Rapids, MI: Zondervan Publishers, 1977), 67.

77. See, e.g., Benjamin B. Warfield, *The Inspiration and Authority of the Bible* (Phillipsburg, NJ: Presbyterian and Reformed, 1948); John Wenham, *Christ and the Bible* (Downers Grove, IL: InterVarsity, 1973), chs. 1–2, 5, and his chapter in Geisler, ed., *Inerrancy*, 3-38; Pierre Ch. Marcel, "Our Lord's Use of Scripture," in Carl F.H. Henry, ed., *Revelation and the Bible* (Grand